Buying and Selling Silver Bullion Like a Pro

By Doug West

Buying and Selling Silver Bullion Like a Pro
Copyright © 2014 Doug West

All Rights Reserved. No part of this book may be reproduce in any form without written permission from the author. Reviewers may quote brief passages in reviews.

Disclaimer and FTC Notice

This book is for educational purposes only and any financial decisions you make should be discussed with your Financial Advisor. The views expressed are those of the author alone, and should not be taken as expert instruction or commands. The reader is responsible for his or her own actions. The author and publisher assumes no financial responsibility for gains or losses you may experience buying or selling precious metals. Efforts have been made to make the information in this book as complete and accurate as possible. However, there may be typographical and content mistakes. Because of this, the book should be used as a general guide and not as the ultimate sources of the subject matter covered.

Table of Contents

Preface 2

Introduction 4

Chapter 1 Why Own Silver 5

Chapter 2 History of Silver, Supply, and Demand 7

Chapter 3 Uses of Silver 11

Chapter 4 The Volatile Price of Silver and How to Profit 16

Chapter 5 Types of Bullion Silver 21

Chapter 6 Where to Buy and Sell Silver 32

Conclusion 36

Addendum 37

References 41

About the author: 42

Preface

Thank you for purchasing this book. I hope it really helps you when it comes to learning the ins and outs of buying silver bullion. I wrote this book to help people understand what silver bullion is and how it is traded. As a coin shop owner, I speak with people daily about silver and hear many interesting stories about what is going on in the world of precious metals. Like nearly all things that involve money, there are those individuals that like to create a hype or buzz about a subject in hopes that you will spend your money with them. That is fine, but it does create a lot of mis-information about buying and selling silver bullion. I wanted to provide clear information that will help when it comes time to buy and sell silver bullion.

In Chapter 1, I go over some of the basic reasons why you would want to own silver. Is it a good long-term investment and is it right for you? Next, I go over a brief history of silver and the supply and demand picture. After reading this chapter, you will probably be surprised at just how useful silver is and how many of the products you use every day contain silver.

Nearly everyday someone asks me the question "what is the best form of silver to own?" In Chapter 5, I answer that question. I discuss some of the most common forms of silver that are regularly bought and sold all over the world and discuss the pros and cons of each type.

So where can I get some silver bullion to get started? Once I have some silver how do I sell it with out being ripped off? These are two very good questions that are answered in Chapter 6. There are many ways to buy and sell silver, and some methods are better than others. Whether you go on the internet or shop locally, you need to have a basic understanding of bullion to minimize your risk of being taken.

This is a short book but it is packed full of useful information that will help you get started in the world of silver bullion.

Introduction

Are you tired of hearing other people talk about buying and selling silver bullion and not having a clue about what they are talking about? Now is your chance to get started in the world of silver investing. Silver, like gold, has been a medium of exchange and a store of value for at least 6,000 years. Not a bad track record! It's not that complicated. You just need a bit of information and a willingness to learn and then you can give it a try. In this book, I take the mystery out of the world of physical silver bullion investing and help you get started.

Chapter 1
Why Own Silver

There are many answers to the question as to why you would want to own silver. Some people own silver to preserve their wealth. Silver has long functioned as a hedge against inflation. For the last few years the official government inflation rates have been low - in the one to three percent per year range. Back in the decades of the 1970's and 1980's there were years where the inflation rate was over ten percent per year. A high inflation rate means that prices rise rapidly which quickly outpaces income growth. This leads to a lower standard of living. Though inflation has been low for the last few years it is still a real fear in many people's minds. Governments all over the world have been printing tremendous amounts of paper money in the last few years, which is not backed by any tangible asset. Eventually, all this excess cash sloshing around in the world's money systems will result in an increase in prices. To help put this in perspective I give this simple example to my customers nearly everyday. Back in 1964, which was the last year the United States put silver in the regular issue coinage, a quarter would buy a gallon of gasoline. Now in 2014, a silver quarter will still has the buying power to purchase that same gallon of gas. This is an example of how silver keeps up with inflation and preserves your buying power.

The above ground supply of silver has dropped to historically low levels in the last 50 years. By the end of the 1950's it is estimated that there was 10 billion ounces of silver surplus. Fast forward to today and that supply has dropped 90 percent to around one billion ounces. As you will see later in this book that is only one years' worth of demand. The supply and demand equation is very tight and a small increase in the demand for silver could have a large impact on the price.

The demand for silver has been growing year after year due to new uses of the metal being discovered. Silver has proven to be a very useful metal and it is used in virtually every part of modern life. The supply of silver coming out of the ground is increasing at a rate below the rate of use – this normally leads to higher prices for silver. It just makes sense to own a commodity with a growing number of uses and only a slowly increasing supply.

In Chapter 4, I get into some details on buying and selling silver bullion so you can trade profitably. As you will see, the price of silver is very volatile and can have large swings up or down in a matter of a few months. There are ways to minimize the pain the price goes down dramatically and take some profits on the way up. You have to have a long-term perspective with silver to increase your chances of trading the metal profitably.

Chapter 2
History of Silver, Supply, and Demand

Silver has been an essential part of human civilization for thousands of years. Apart from its significance as a valuable precious metal, it has also been a very popular form of currency. The word Silver comes from the Latin word *argentum*. As far as the usage of silver as a form of currency is concerned, the ancient Greeks were known to use silver ingots for trading purposes approximately 4000 years ago.

The Old Testament of the Bible refers to surface mining of silver and its separation from lead in the islands of Aegean Sea as well as in areas around Asia Minor. This indicates that silver was known to these ancient civilizations as old as the fourth millennium BC. Moreover, before the discovery of the New World and its vast silver reserves, the miners of the Roman Empire were engaged in massive production of silver because their currency was heavily dependent on a steady silver metal supply. Historians believe that around 10,000 tons of silver stock was in circulation in mid second century AD in the Roman economy.

The Chinese Empire used silver to trade silk, opium, tea and porcelain, etc. with the western world. Later on, the influx of Spanish bullion from the New World led to the establishment of a silver standard that remained the basis of monetary systems until the 20th century.

Silver coins have been one of the oldest and most popular forms of coinage produced. Although there is a difference between the currency coins and silver bullion coins (used as a form of investment), yet they both form an important part of history of monetary systems around the world. Until recent times, silver was an integral part of nearly all coinage systems throughout the world.

Silver Mine Production

Only about a third of the silver mined in the world comes from silver mines and the rest is a by-product from mining other metals. Mexico is the leading producer of silver. Peru, China, Australia, and Russia are next four top producing countries of silver. The United States in ninth on the list of silver producing countries. In 2013, the total world mine production was 819.6 million ounces. Each year the world's mines increase the output of silver by slightly over two percent. The average cost of mining silver is about $10 an ounce.

The top five silver producing companies in 2013 were:

1. Fesnillo plc. Based in Mexico is the largest producer of silver ore (primary silver) and Mexico's second largest producer of gold. The company operates three gold and silver mines in Mexico.

2. BHP Billiton plc in Australia. This is a multi-national metals and petroleum mining corporation that is the world's largest mining company based on 2013 revenues.

3. KGHM Plska Miedz S.A. in Poland. This company is a major producer of copper and silver with operations in Poland, Chile, United States and Canada.

4. Clencore Xstrata plc. Based in Switzerland is a multi-national corporation specializing in commodity trading and mining.

5. Goldcorp Inc. is a Canadian based mining company. The company has gold and silver mines in Canada, U.S.A., Mexico, Central America, and South America.

The largest United States based producer of silver is Coeur Mining. Coeur ranks tenth in the world and is involved in mining of gold and silver in the United States, Mexico, and various countries in South America.

Silver Supply

In addition to mining, which is responsible for 84 percent of the total supply, silver also comes from recycling in the form of scrap. According to the *World Silver Survey 2014* the year 2013 saw a large drop in the above ground supply of scrap silver. This was due to the lower silver price and an exhaustion of the scrap supply. This supply comes from the melting of old coins and jewelry sold for their bullion value. Because of the decrease in scrap silver the total from this source has dropped to below 20 percent of the total supply of yearly silver. Another lesser source of silver comes from governments selling portions of their silver supply to raise money. This is a small portion of the above-ground silver supply. The change in the supply from governments increased slightly from 2012 to 2013. Based on all the sources of silver, there was a small drop in the available silver supply from 1,052 million ounces to 1,019 million ounces. This decrease in supply lead to a small physical silver deficit during the year of 2013.

Silver Demand

The demand for silver is broken down into three parts: industrial, jewelry, and investment. These three categories represent 95 percent of the annual silver demand. In 2013, the total physical demand for silver was a record 1,081 million ounces. The largest component of this demand came from the industrial sector which is over half the total demand. In 2013, this demand was slightly down at 586.6 million ounces. Projections are that the industrial demand for silver will grow at approximately a rate of five percent per year. The second area of demand for silver is for jewelry and décor. There was an increase in the use for silver in the jewelry industry. This was a result of an increase of retail sales for jewelry. The third area of demand comes from silver being used as an investment vehicle. Some examples from this area include Exchange Traded Funds, silver coins, and medallions. On the average, the world's demand for silver increase approximately 27 million ounces per year.

Chapter 3
Uses of Silver

Whether you know it or not silver plays a part in your life. As you will see in the sections below, silver enters our lives in various forms in many areas of our lives.

Electronics and Electrical:

The electronics and electrical industries have taken broad advantage of the fact that silver has the highest electrical conductivity of any metal. Silver is used in brazing and soldering of electrical components together allowing both a mechanical and electrical connection. Because silver does not corrode the way many other metals do, it is used in electrical switches. For example, look at all the electrical switches that are in an automobile – you turn on and off the radio, air-conditioner, and heater; the electrical windows go up and down, you open the trunk lid from inside the car, plus many more. Even certain high-end ear phones utilize silver for better music quality. The use of silver in mobile phones has greatly increased the demand of silver. Just about every electronic device you see today contains some form of silver.

According to the Silver Institute's 2014 report, *The Outlook for New Electric and Electrical Uses of Silver* the industrial demand picture for silver looks bright. There are several new areas (and some mature areas) of technology that are growing and taking silver along for the ride. The authors of the report are projecting a five percent growth in the industrial demand for silver. This is significant since the industrial sector is already the largest demand sector for silver.

Take a walk around nearly any neighborhood in America and you notice solar cells on the roofs of houses and commercial building. Solar Cells that are part of the larger group of electrical devices termed photovoltaics, which convert sunlight into electricity. Projections are that the use of photovoltaics worldwide will continue to increase and thus more silver will be required.

Another new growth area for the use of silver is Flexible Electronics, which is a broad area of electronic devices. Currently your computer or smart phone screen is made from hard rigid materials. This rigidity imposes design constraints on the overall device. A more flexible screen allows the devices to be more closely associated with the movement of the human body. The key part of this technology is the use of silver nanowire. An ideal nanowire is a few tens of a nanometer in diameter and a few micrometers in length. To give you some prospective, a piece of paper is 100,000 nanometers thick and a human hair is about 90,000 nanometers wide. This allows electronic devices to be integrated into clothing. Many of these devices are just reaching the market and this area appears poised for rapid growth.

Electrical lighting is slowly changing from near universal reliance on the incandescent light to other forms of lighting such as, the compact florescent light and Light Emitting Diodes (LEDs). Silver is a fundamental component in the LED. LEDs have three significant advantages of incandescent lights: First is the efficiency, you can produce much more light from an LED per unit of electricity consumed when compared to older lighting technology. Secondly, the life of an LED light is years, rather than months for an incandescent light. Lastly, LEDs are more mechanically resilient. The older style glass bulbs are rather easy to break. I know I have broken my share of light bulbs in my lifetime. LED lights are tougher and can withstand more of the bumps and bruises life has to offer. All of the beneficial features of the LED lights has led to a rapid incorporation of this technology into everyday lighting. In 2013, LEDs make up approximately 20 percent of the lighting market. By the end of 2014 this percent is expected to be 30 percent.

Jewelry:

Silver jewelry has been very common since ancient times. Silver being very ductile makes it perfect for jewelry. It is in demand even today as silver jewelry is very fashionable.

Silverware:

Although the term silverware can be quite generic, being used to describe kitchen utensils such as spoons, plates and knives, the term was generally used for those implements that were made from silver. Such was the popularity of the use of silver for making cutlery, a practice still commonly used. Due to the introduction of new materials, the use of silver in flatware has decreased.

Photography:

Compounds of silver salts with halogens or silver nitrates are sensitive to light and have formed the basis of photography for over 100 years. With the advent of digital photography, its use in this field are dwindling. The demand for silver in photography has gone from 179 million ounces in 2004 down to 50 million ounces in 2013. Currently the percent of silver demand for photography is less than five percent and appears to have stabilized.

X-rays and other radiographic diagnostics:

X-ray films also utilize silver halides. These silver salts upon processing impart the black color to an X-ray. The salt in the places on the film not exposed to radiations washes away during processing. With digital X-ray cameras becoming more and more commonplace, the use of silver based films in radiography has declined over the years.

Batteries:

Silver has begun replacing lithium commonly used in batteries. Lithium had hazardous effects if it leaked out of the batteries and hence a substitute for it was necessary. Most silver batteries of recent times completely eschew flammable liquids making them much safer.

Chemistry and Electroplating:

Silver and silver salts are used for a variety of experiments taught to students in high school. They are also used as a catalyst that hastens many other reactions without itself interfering in the reaction. The electrodes for electrolysis are usually silver plated. Its ease of deposition makes silver ideal for electroplating.

Windows:

The reflective properties of silver keeps out more than 60 percent of heat from sunrays which would enter a window without the silver coating. This reduces the energy spent by air-conditioners to cool homes and offices.

Medical:

Silver has been used extensively in medical remedies from China and other parts of the world for millennia. The early pioneers in North America would place silver coins in water and milk storage barrels to inhibit spoilage. By 1800, it was common practice to store water, milk, wine, and vinegar in silver vessels to increase their useful life. The anti-bacterial properties of silver were not understood at that time but the beneficial effects were apparent. Today, silver is used in antibacterial creams in the form of silver sulfadiazene, a sulfur compound. It is also used to coat endotracheal tubes and urinary catheters. Silver stains are used to view many bacteria under the microscope such as spirochetes.

Coins and Medals:

Coins have been made of silver since 400 BC and continues today. Nearly all government monetary systems up until the 1960's were based in some fashion around silver and gold. Due to the rising price of silver most of the governments around the world stopped using silver in their regular coins for circulation. At that time, this was a big source of silver demand. It was not until the 1980's when mints all over the world started producing silver coins again as commemorative or bullion issues. They were taking advantage of the growth in silver investment and were providing a method for individuals to accumulate silver. In 2000, 32.1 million ounces of silver were used to make coins and medals, by 2009 that number had over doubled to 78.7 million ounces. In addition to silver investors, there are tens of thousands of coin collectors, called numismatists, who collect and invest in old silver coins for their beauty, history, and profit potential.

Chapter 4
The Volatile Price of Silver and How to Profit

It would be an understatement to say the price of silver is volatile, meaning, it is constantly changing and the price can change dramatically in the course of a few short weeks. The volatile nature of the price of silver is a blessing and a curse. If the price did not fluctuate, there would not be an opportunity to buy and sell at a profit. Of course, the trick is to buy when the price is low and sell when it is higher. No one gets this right all the time. To successfully speculate in silver or any other item you just need to be right more times than you are wrong. There are some basic tools and strategies you can use to cope with the volatile nature of the price of silver.

One basic tool that you have in your arsenal to combat the volatile nature of the price of silver is Dollar Cost Averaging (DCA). This is really a simple idea that can significantly improve your results. Dollar Cost Averaging means that you buy a fixed dollar amount of silver on a regular basis rather than one large purchase. Say you have $10,000.00 at your disposal and you want to get into silver. Each month go out and buy $1000.00 worth of silver. Unless you just get lucky with a one-time purchase when the price is low using DCA will result in your average price per ounce being lower than one time single purchase over the same period.

This next tool is probably the hardest one to implement, that is, patience. The silver market moves in long term cycles and there is a lot of short term volatility along the way. Don't expect the market to jump up just because you have made a large purchase. Develop your mental attitude that this is a long term investment and you won't be trading on a daily or weekly basis. I tell my customers in the coin shop that if you are not planning on holding the silver for at least five years you are increasing your chances of loss. There are always "experts" hyping silver and gold telling you that the price is getting ready to take off. Think long-term and don't listen to a salesman's pitch. Time is on your side.

People have a trait in that they are risk averse. That is, we would rather avoid a loss than possibly obtain a gain. The way this plays out in the silver market is that people get very leery of purchasing silver when the price is dropping, and it can do this for many weeks or months in a row. It is no fun telling your friends the value of your investment is falling. Have you ever heard a gambler bragging about the many times they lost money at the casino? No, you only hear about the infrequent wins. This is where DCA and patience comes in – stick to your plan. I know this is extremely hard advice to follow – I have failed myself on occasion. Another aspect of human's nature to be risk averse is that we tend to jump on whatever is going up in price. Once the price of silver starts moving up there is a lot more interest which generates more buyers which drives the price up. When your friend, who does not have a clue about silver, tells you that you need to be buying silver then that should be a queue to you that maybe you should start taking a profit on the silver you accumulated on the way down.

Figure 1 – 10 Year Chart of the Price of Silver (courtesy www.kitco.com)

So when is a good time to sell the silver that you have accumulated? The short answer is to sell at a profit – sounds easy! Two factors to consider when it comes to selling are when to sell and how much profit to take. One clear signal when it comes time to start selling is when there is a frenzy and the prices are moving up week after week. When it comes to selling, you want to use a process similar to Dollar Cost Averaging except you are selling rather than buying. You start selling a part of your position each month. If the upward trend continues for many months, you may end up liquating your entire hoard at a profit. If the upward trend is short term and only lasts a few months then you have liquidated on a small portion of your holding. Either way, you have made a profit on what you have sold. Hold your cash and roll it into the next down trend using DCA.

One other tool you have to help you profit from the volatile nature of the price of silver is the mild seasonal price trends. A seasonal trend is when some feature of a market tends to repeat year after year. I use the term "mild" seasonal trend for silver because they do not always repeat. An example of a seasonal trend is in the stock market embodied in the adage "Sell in May and go away". Stocks tend to have a seasonal trend where most of the yearly gains occur in the first two quarters of the year. This too is not always correct. So how do you use seasonal trends in silver to take profits and mitigate down side risk? Here are some features of the silver price you want to understand.

1. The first two months of year tend to see the price of silver move up. This is not a given but you can use it to your advantage. It is not as simple as buy in December and sell in March. If it is time for you to start the selling process and you see a short-term low in December and the price starts moving up in January this may be an indication that the seasonal trend is in play and you may want to sell into it.

2. March through June tend to be months that do not see much price appreciation. These are generally good months to add to your position.

3. The remainder of the year is rather mixed with a slight uptrend. July is the month with the highest probability of an up move in the second half of the year.

In addition to seasonal trends silver tends to follow gold to a certain extent. If gold is moving up then silver will not be too far behind and just the opposite is true as well. If gold is dropping silver will normally be right behind it. Do not fight the relationship between gold and silver – use it to your advantage. Use gold to confirm your plan for buying or selling silver.

Both gold and silver function somewhat as an alternative currency to the major currencies of the world, such as, the U.S. dollar, European Union Euro, Great Britain Pound, and the Japanese Yen. Gold functions more in this role than does silver. When the United States dollar is strengthening relative to the other world major currencies, such as, the Euro, Pound, and Yen, then expect gold and silver to be weaker. The opposite is true when the U.S. dollar is weakening then expect the price of silver to be firm or rise.

Chapter 5
Types of Bullion Silver

There are different types of silver bullion and each has its advantages and disadvantages. One of the oldest forms of silver commonly traded is old U.S. coins made from 90 percent silver. These coins were minted before 1965 and are sometimes called "Junk" silver. Probably the most popular form of silver bullion comes in the form of the one Troy ounce silver American Silver Eagle. These lovely coins have been minted by the U.S. mint since 1986. They sell at a slightly higher premium over other types of silver. Other countries, such as, Canada, Austria, Australia, and Mexico produce silver bullion coins that are also very popular with collectors and investors. Private mints, such as SilverTowne, APMEX, Johnson Matthey, Sunshine Mining, and many more produce silver bullion in many forms that are commonly traded. In this chapter, we will take a more detailed look at each of the forms of silver bullion and see which one(s) might work for you.

U.S. Silver Coins

Figure 2 – U.S. 90 Percent Silver Coins

Before silver bars and rounds became popular in the late 1970's silver traders bought and sold United States 90 percent silver coins as a form of bullion. These are dimes, quarters, halves, and dollars issued before 1965. In this section I go over some of the common types of U.S. silver coins that you would run into when buying and selling silver. If you are very lucky, you just might find one of these silver coins in your change.

Silver Content of U.S. Coins

Before you get serious about buying and selling silver coins you really need to know just how much silver is in each type of silver coin. Table 1 lists the actual silver content of each type of coin. As a coin circulates, the silver wears down and, the actual silver weight of the coin slightly decreases. The silver content in Table 1 is for a freshly minted coin; however, the silver contents listed below are still useful for buying and selling.

Table 1 - Silver Content of US Coins

Denomination Troy Ounces of Silver per Coin
Dimes (pre 1965) 0.0723
Quarters (pre 1965) 0.1808
Halves (pre 1965) 0.3616
Halves (1965-1970) 0.1479
Dollars (pre 1936) 0.7734

As an example to illustrate how to use Table 1, suppose you are buying a roll (40 coins) of silver Washington quarters. These all should date before 1965. Here is how to calculate the silver value of the roll. If silver is a $30.00 dollars per ounce on the Spot market, then the roll is worth 40*0.1808*$30.00 = $216.96. This is the melt value of the roll when silver is at $30.00 per Troy ounce. You will probably have to pay more than $216.96 to purchase the roll. Normally the premium would be five to ten percent over the melt value. If you are selling the roll to a dealer expect to get five to ten percent less than the melt value of the roll. The difference between the buy and sell price for the dealer is his/her profit.

Dealers normally quote the price of 90 percent silver coins on a "times face value" method. To calculate this assume silver is at $30.00 per Troy ounce. Take 30 times 0.723 and this gives the multiplier 21.69. For a $10 roll of silver quarters the melt value is $10 x 21.69 = $216.90. The number 0.723 is the number of Troy ounces of silver in one dollar face value of United States 90 silver dimes, quarters, and half dollars. Note this is the same amount we calculated in the above example. Many dealers use a multiplier of 0.715 instead of 0.723 to take into account the fact that the coins have wear and they do not have as much silver as they did when they were minted. Dealers need to make a living so they will buy the silver at, say 20 times face and sell the silver coins at 23 times face. Each dealer has his or her own buy/sell spread. The buy/sell spread is subject to change as the supply and demand picture changes for silver bullion.

Buying and selling silver in the form of U.S. 90 percent silver coins is a very good method to trade silver. The premium between the buy and sell price is normally reasonable and you get the added advantage of having old coins to look at and enjoy. One of the disadvantages is the supply of 90 percent silver coins is limited. It is common knowledge in the coin collector community that approximately 90 percent of the U.S. silver coins have been melted for their silver content. Dealers may or may not have inventory at any given time to meet your needs. Remember, these coins were last made in 1964 and can sometimes be hard to locate in a large quantity.

Morgan and Peace Silver Dollars

Figure 3 – Morgan and Peace Silver Dollars

The Morgan dollar was minted from 1878 until 1921 and in lower grades they can trade near their bullion value. These coins are very popular with collectors and high grade uncirculated coins sell for many thousands of dollars. The Morgan dollars that trade near their bullion value are called "culls". A cull dollar will have heavy wear (partial rims, partial date or legends), some damage (dings, scratches, etc.), and can have some corrosion which makes them turn unusual colors. Due to the popularity of these dollars even the cull dollars trade over their bullion value. If you are selling cull Morgan dollars to a dealer they should at least give you the melt value. If silver is $30.00 per Troy ounce then the melt value of the Morgan dollar is 0.7734*$30 = $23.20. If you are buying cull Morgan dollars from a dealer expect to pay $2 to $3 over their melt value per coin.

In 1921, the design of the Morgan dollar was changed to commemorate the end of World War I. This new dollar was called the Peace dollar. The Peace dollar contains the same amount of silver as the Morgan dollar and the cull dollars trade for about the same price as the cull Morgan dollars. When you come across Peace dollars, you normally see the dates 1922, 1923, and 1924. These are high mintage dates and represent the bulk of the total mintage of the coinage for this series. Dates from 1927 to 1935 are less common and typically do not trade near their bullion value unless they are damaged or have heavy wear.

Like the dimes, quarters, and half dollars made from 90 percent silver the low grade Morgan and Peace dollars are a good way to accumulate silver. They also suffer from the same limitation as the smaller denomination coins, that is, sometimes they are hard to locate in any quantity and the premium can be a little more pricy than you should be paying. One real advantage they do have is protection from down side price risk. Since silver dollars are such a popular coin they also have a collector or numismatic value. The collector value acts to cushion the price when the price of silver drops significantly. When silver is low, say less than $20.00 per Troy ounce, the premium for cull dollars increases and you can normally sell them for well over their melt value. When silver is rising the premium to their melt value will decrease but the value of the dollar will still increase due to their silver value.

American Silver Eagles

Figure 4 – American Silver Eagles

The American Silver Eagle is one of the world's most popular silver bullion coins. The U.S. Mint started production of this coin back in 1986 and minting continues today. Silver collectors and investors actively seek this coin for their collections. The coin features Lady Liberty walking in the sunset on the obverse (front) of the coin and has an eagle on the reverse (back). The coin contains one Troy ounce of 999 fine silver. Normally, the Eagles sell for $3.00 to $4.00 over their melt value. Dealers normally pay their melt value or a $1.00 over melt to purchase the coins from the public.

Not all the dates of American Silver Eagles sell for close to their bullion value. The 1996 is the low mintage date for the uncirculated bullion Eagles with just over 3.6 million minted. The 1996 Eagles sell for a $30.00 to $40.00 premium over melt value. There are several other dates such as the 1986, 1994, 1995, 2006-W, and 2007-W Eagles that command a significant premium over melt as well. As a rule, if you are buying American Silver Eagles for their bullion content you will be getting mainly coins minted within the last ten years.

American Silver Eagles are an excellent way to accumulate silver bullion. They are readily available in quantity and dealers are more than willing to buy and sell the Eagles. One thing to be cautious about regarding the Eagles is the premium can vary depending on supply and demand. If the spot silver price is where you want it, December and January are typically good months to sell Eagles since the premium is usually higher in these months. These months typically have higher premiums due to the Christmas season purchasing and the end of the yearly production for the U.S. Mint. The change in premium over melt is usually small and the main factor would be the underlying price of silver bullion. If the price is right, any month of the year can be a good time to sell at a profit.

Silver Bars and Rounds

Figure 5 – One Troy Ounce Silver Rounds made of 999 Fine Silver

Another form of silver commonly traded is 999 fine silver bars and rounds. Privately minted silver bars and rounds come in a variety of sizes, everything from a tenth of an ounce to over 100 ounces of silver. Whether you are buying a small quantity or large you want to make sure that the round or bar is marked

"999 Fine Silver" and "One Troy Ounce" or some equivalent statement. The "999 Fine Silver" refers to the purity of the silver, which means, it is 99.9 percent pure silver. Sometimes you will see the abbreviation "F.S." for fine silver. The "One Troy Ounce" lets you know that the bar or round weights at least 31.1 grams, which is a Troy ounce. On any piece of bullion you buy it must be stated the weight and purity. Avoid bullion that is marked "100 mils", this refers to the thickness of the silver plating. The bar or round is most likely copper with a thin plating of silver. If the word "plating" appears on the bullion try to determine if it is silver over copper or gold over silver, or whatever. The best advice is to buy from a reputable dealer that will buy the silver back when it comes time to sell.

A general rule on pricing privately minted silver is the smaller the unit of weight the larger the premium over the melt value. For example, a one Troy ounce 999 fine silver round usually sells for $1.00 to $2.00 over the melt value and a 100 ounce bar may sells as cheap as $0.50 per ounce over the melt value. I normally advise my customers to purchase bars that are less than 20 ounces in total weight. Avoid buying silver rounds or bars that are fractional, meaning, they contain less than one Troy ounce of silver. The premium on fractional silver bars and rounds is just too high if you are a silver investor. Stick with one, five, and ten ounce bars or rounds. When you go to sell your 999 fine silver bullion expect to receive around $1.00 below the melt value to $0.50 over melt value per Troy ounce. If the dealer is offering you less than this then check with another dealer. Due to many factors, dealers all seem to have a slightly different buy/sell spread on their bullion pricing.

World Silver Bullion Coins

Figure 6 – World Silver Bullion Coins

Since the late 1980's many countries around the world have gotten into the action and have started producing silver coins which have become another method to acquire silver. The Canadian Maple Leaf one-ounce 9999 fine silver coin is probably the second most popular bullion related coin traded. The Maple Leaf started production in 1988 and the coins have a $5 denomination. By the late 1990's the Canadian Maple Leaf began adding privy marks, such as, a Tiger, the Titanic, and a Rabbit. This was a way for the Canadian Mint to take advantage of the emerging bullion collectors. The addition of the small privy marks to the coins effectively made a variety to collect and hence more sales for the Canadian Mint. Due to their low mintages, coins with privy marks normally sell for well over their bullion value. For a common date Canadian Maple Leaf one Troy ounce bullion coin expect to pay $3.00 to $4.00 over melt value.

In 1992, Australia introduced the one Troy ounce Kookaburra silver coin with a denomination of $1. These coins normally sell for $5.00 to $10.00 over their bullion value. Each year the design has been changed and the years with lower mintages cause some Kookaburras to sell for a large premium over their bullion value. The Royal Australian mint has also produces the Koala and Kangaroo series of silver bullion coins. Generally, the Australian silver bullion coins should not be purchased as a bullion investment due to the high premium. However, these coins may appreciate nicely in value over time due to their scarcity and the intrinsic value of the silver.

China also produces gold and silver bullion coins.

In 1993, China introduced the Panda series of bullion coins. The coins carry a denomination of 10 Yuan. This series is much like the bullion coins produced by the Royal Australian Mint, in that, the series design changes each year and the mintages have been low. These coins are in high demand and as a result, they are not considered a good vehicle for pure silver bullion investment.

Other commonly seen one ounce bullion coins are the Austria Philharmonic and the Mexico Libertad. These coins typically sell for $3.00 to $4.00 over their melt value and dealers normally pay around their melt value for these coins.

Sterling Silver Flatware and Jewelry

When an item is made of Sterling silver it has a 92.5 percent net silver content with the remainder in base metals like copper. Most silver jewelry is made from Sterling silver and so is some vintage flatware (knives, forks, and spoons). For centuries, silver was the preferred metal in the manufacturing of household kitchen utensils and cutlery. The anti-corrosive and antimicrobial properties of silver made it very useful for this application. As beautiful as silver jewelry can be and as useful as silver flatware can be Sterling silver products do not make a very good investment vehicle for owning silver. There a couple of reasons why this is true. First, items marked Sterling silver may or may not be 92.5 percent silver. Sterling silver is notorious for not being of the stated level of purity. It is common to encounter an item marked "Sterling" or "925" and be made of a heavy silver plate with a copper core. For this reason, dealers tend to discount significantly their buy prices for Sterling silver. The spread between the buy and sell price for Sterling silver is just too high to make it a realistic form of silver to accumulate. Secondly, Sterling comes in many forms, such as, forks, spoons, bowls, knives, cups, platters, and much more. It is certainly easier to store your silver in the form of 999 fine silver or in coins than it is to store these various other forms of Sterling silver.

Chapter 6
Where to Buy and Sell Silver

In the last few years, the world has changed for those interested in investing in gold and silver bullion. The game changer is the internet. Before the internet, the bullion investor only had mail order and local coin shops as sources for bullion. Now you get on your computer or smart phone and just about anything in the world is available to you – including precious metals. So how do you use this new tool to your advantage? The short answer is eBay. I know that eBay had a bad reputation in the early years with shady dealers that would rip you off with counterfeit or

misrepresented products. I have to give eBay credit in that they have really cleaned up their platform and with a little common sense, you can buy and sell silver without too much fear. In addition to the internet, buying and selling with local dealers is still a very viable option.

Buying and Selling Silver on eBay

I am a Platinum level Top Rated Power Seller on eBay (eBay ID: dwest61506) so I have a large amount of experience with eBay. Over the years, I have bought hundreds and hundreds of coins and bullion on eBay and sold many thousands of items (mostly coins and bullion) on eBay. Listed below are tips for the buyer and seller to make your time on eBay more enjoyable and profitable.

Tips for buying silver on eBay

- Get your account setup and make a few small purchases to gain feedback and experience. Many dealers on eBay will not accept bids from people with zero or only a small number of feedbacks.

- You will probably have better luck finding silver bargains by bidding on auctions. There are several sellers on eBay that run auctions for silver bullion items on a daily basis and I know from experience that not all auctions are profitable for the seller. You just need to be diligent and bid only what you are willing to pay. Do not get emotional about the auction. Bid your maximum and wait and see what happens. I bid on many auctions and I probably only get one out of ten. I bid cheap and do not get in a competition with other bidders. Very seldom does silver sell on eBay for less than a 10 percent premium over the melt value.

- Buy from proven sellers with a lot of positive feedback. These would be the Power Sellers and/or Top Rated Sellers. You want to be buying from people that have a proven record of accomplishment and know what they are doing.

- Most Top Rated Power Sellers offer a 14 day return privilege. However, this is not always the case for sellers of precious metals. The sellers do not want to accept the risk of the price of silver dropping once you receive your silver and then you return it to them. There are a few sellers on eBay (including myself) that offer a full 14 day return privilege even on purchases of precious metals.

Seek out sellers that offer the return privilege. This just gives you another option.

Tips for selling silver on eBay

- Just like above, get your account setup and make a few small purchases to gain feedback and experience. Buyers on eBay are very leery about buying from sellers with only a few feedbacks. A simple way to get feedbacks quickly as a seller is to sell a few items slightly below the current market price or start a small silver related auction at 99 cents. eBay has a three month probation period which limits your sales volume and dollar amount so if you are thinking about selling on eBay then get started now.

- When making your listings on eBay you want to be very clear on what you are selling. Most of the buyers are very savvy so you want to give them all the information they need to make a purchase or bid on your auction.

- In the early days of eBay taking good pictures was more of a problem. Now, even a relatively inexpensive smart phone can take a good picture of your silver. Just like the wording in the text of your listing the pictures need to reflect exactly what is up for auction or for sale in the Buy-It-Now format.

Buying and Selling Silver Locally

If you are not comfortable buying and selling silver bullion over the internet there are many options to buy and sell locally. Coin Shops have always been the place where people go to buy and sell precious metals. I am a coin shop co-owner and we buy and sell precious metals on a daily basis. Not all coin shops operate on the same business model. In our shop, we publish a daily buy/sell spread for different forms of precious metals. This makes it easy for customers when they want to buy or sell silver. Recently silver was at $20.00 per Troy ounce and we were buying one Troy ounce of 999 fine silver bars and rounds for $19.50 each and were selling the same items for $21.40. This is a normal buy/sell spread. Search for dealers in your area that can quote to you their buy and sell prices for common types of silver bullion. Check your Yellow Pages or perform an internet search for dealers near you. Remember, the dealers that have the biggest advertising budget may not have the best buy/sell spread for precious metals. You, the customer pay for this big advertising budget. It really pays to shop around with your local shops to get the best deals.

Another common way to put buyers and sellers together is Craigslist.org. We advertise regularly on Craigslist and it is effective for bringing customers into our Coin Shop. As an individual wanting to buy or sell silver with another individual over Craigslist I would be very leery of purchasing silver from people you don't know anything about. My customers have told me many stories about their adventures using Craigslist and most of them are not positive. Until you have gained a lot of experience with silver, I would recommend avoiding Craigslist.

Many Pawn Shops will buy and sell silver and other precious metals. I have not had much luck with Pawn Shops when it comes to silver. Either they did not have any available for sale or what they did have was overpriced. I am sure there are Pawn Shops out there that are good to work with but this will be the exception rather than the rule.

Conclusion

By now, hopefully you have a better idea about how to buy and sell silver. The long-term supply and demand numbers paint a picture of a precious metal that has a limited supply and has an increasing demand. All the "easy" silver to mine in the world has been found. All that is left is silver buried deep within the earth, which is very expensive to remove and process. There are many different forms of silver bullion. Pick the type(s) that are right for you and start by making a few purchases. Learning by doing is the one of the best ways to gain experience. Spend some time looking for a good dealer that is available to answer your questions and one that will have a low spread between their buy/sell prices. Do not forget to use one of the big advantages you now have, which is the internet and eBay. This makes it so much easier to buy and sell silver bullion compared to what it was just 20 years ago. Buying your silver at regular intervals and spending the same dollar amount each time, or dollar cost averaging, allows you to reduce your overall cost per ounce. This is a great way to accumulate silver. Finally, be patient. Silver prices are very volatile and the supply and demand realities sometimes take years to play out. Do not get caught up in all the hype when silver prices are very high and make some foolish purchases.

I hope this book has been beneficial and I wish the best of luck in your endeavor to buy and sell silver bullion like a professional. Thank you for reading this book!

Addendum

Since this book was published in the summer of 2014, things have changed in a significant way in the silver market; for this reason, I wanted to give an update at the end of 2014 on the silver bullion market.

Price. As you can see in figure 6, the price of silver continues to drop. As of December 2014, it is at a five-year low. There are a variety of reasons for the price slide, including that the stock market is at a record high and money keeps flowing into stocks. When money flows into the stock market, it is diverted away from alternative investments such as precious metals. This trend will continue until investors figure out that the stock market is overpriced and is due for a serious correction. Another contributing factor is the strength of the U.S. Dollar index. Right now, the dollar is enjoying great favor among currency traders all over the world. A strong dollar means lower prices for precious metals. An additional factor driving down the price of silver is the weakness of the price of oil. At first glance, you would not think that the price of oil and silver are correlated, but they are to some extent. In late November, the Organization of Petroleum Countries (OPEC) met and decided to keep oil production at current levels. This high level of production has caused a surplus of oil on world markets, and the price is at a multi-year low. A slightly lower industrial demand has also depressed prices. As you will read shortly, the supply and demand picture is not rosy and this has also depressed prices.

Figure 7 - 10 Year Chart of the Price of Silver (courtesy www.kitco.com)

Supply. In early November, the U.S. Mint abruptly discontinued minting of the American Silver Eagle bullion coin. The Mint stated that it had sold all the Eagles available for distribution. The demand had outpaced the supply, and they just could not keep up with the demand for the Silver Eagles. A couple of weeks later, the Mint resumed production of the Silver Eagles on a limited basis. This year's production is projected to be over 42 million ounces. If not a record production level, it will be close to the peak production year. This abrupt supply disruption of silver into the market caused the premium on Eagles to increase nearly a dollar over the existing premium.

The low price of silver is causing supply disruptions all over the country. When silver prices were higher, I could call and order hundreds or thousands of ounces of silver and have it in my shop in a few days. Now not all forms of silver are readily available, and there can be a lengthy waiting period for silver bullion. This situation is very similar to what happened during the Great Recession in 2008 and 2009. Then price of silver dipped below $10 per Troy ounce and people stopped selling silver and it was nearly impossible to get your hands on any significant quantity of silver in the form of 999 fine rounds or bars. In my coin shop, the number of silver buyers outnumber the seller by at least ten to one. The only sellers right now are the individuals who just need the money, or those that are liquidating an estate and also just want the money right now.

According to a report prepared by Thomson Reuters GFMS for the Silver Institute, the supply of silver is projected to increase for 2014 by nearly 3% year-over-year. The mines in Guatemala, Mexico, Chile, and Peru have been producing at near record rates and the total amount of silver mined has increased. In 2014, the amount of silver coming onto the market from the scrap recovery is expected to drop by 14%. The increase in the mine production is greater than the decrease in scrap recovery, so there will more silver available in 2014 when compared to 2013.

Demand. Like the supply picture for silver, the sources of demand also paints a muddled picture. According to the Thomson Reuters GFMS report previously referenced, the industrial demand is expect to be down nearly 2% for the year. This is a result of the slowing world economic activity, and thus a reduced demand for silver in products. The demand for silver coins and bullion rounds and bars has been strong during the last quarter of 2014. The falling prices have brought bullion buyers back into the market. The holdings of silver in Exchange Traded Funds (ETFs) has slightly increased in 2014, to approximately 650 million ounces. Overall, the total demand for physical silver is expected to be down in 2014, year-over-year.

Summary. When will all this bad news for silver bullion change? Who knows for sure, but one thing is for certain, things always change. Remember, investing in silver is a long-term proposition. When the price is low, it is a good time to accumulate bullion. Based on the supply and demand numbers, 2015 is looking like it could be a repeat of 2014, that is, side ways to lower prices. The current dark cloud over silver will one day lift and it will be back in favor again, and the price will rise in a dramatic fashion.

References

C&D Coins eBay Store http://stores.ebay.com/C-D-Coins-and-Currency

Current silver price and precious metals news www.kitco.com

The Silver Institute https://www.silverinstitute.org/site/

Coin World Almanac Eighth Edition by the Staff of Coin World, Published by Amos Press, Inc. Sidney, OH, 2011

About the author:

Doug West is the senior numismatist at the family owned business C&D Coins in Raymore, Missouri. Doug has over four decades of experience as a coin collector and dealer and has been involved in numerous numismatic organizations over the years. He is author of several coin related articles, eBooks, and maintains the web site www.canddcoins.com. Stay in touch by following Doug on Twitter at @DCoins.

NOTES

Printed in Dunstable, United Kingdom